Needles, threads, scissors, a thimble, pins, and a frame; linen, rayon, taffeta, velvet, or tweed—these are some of the materials of the embroiderer. This book teaches the basic stitches, and suggests many ways to design a pattern: how to plan shapes, and colors; how to keep a sketchbook; what to look for in museums, at the zoo, and in nature.

A

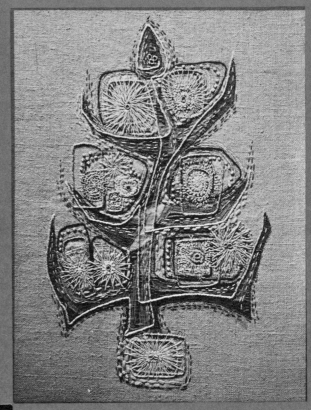

B

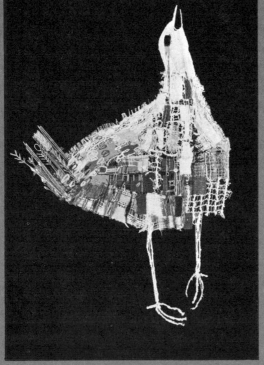

C

A. Animal—Chinese. (Embroiderers' Guild Collection).
B. Cross Section II. Linen, net and stitchery applied to hessian. (Jan Beaney).
C. Seagull. Applied nets and curtain fabrics. (Pat Ross).
D. Detail Syon Cope. English, late 13th century. Silk and silver-gilt threads. (Victoria and Albert Museum. Crown Copyright).
E. Detail from shawl — Indian. (Embroiderers' Guild Collection).
F. Woman's tunic. English, late 16th century. Some couched work. (Victoria and Albert Museum. Crown Copyright).

D

E

F

Library of Congress Catalog Card No. 67-24708

Copyright © 1966 Kaye & Ward Ltd

Reprinted 1968

All Rights Reserved

Printed in Great Britain

The Young Embroiderer

1. Detail of panel 'Minerva'. Applied materials—hand and machine embroidery, some quilting and padded work. (Jean Baker).

THE YOUNG

EMBROIDERER

A how-it-is-done book of embroidery
by
Jan Beaney

Frederick Warne & Co., Inc.
NEW YORK AND LONDON

Table of Contents

Introduction

2. Cut paper patterns.

This book is about embroidery and how you can learn to be your own designer. If you like a variety of materials, rich colour, texture and pattern, you will find this craft very exciting.

It would be difficult for you to complete an embroidered panel successfully without at first making experiments with shape, colour, texture and stitchery. Therefore, the book is divided into sections, each dealing with an aspect of the craft. You will probably enjoy doing the exercises and if they should be successful in their own right; you could always mount them as cards, calendars or tiny pictures. These colourful decorations, if displayed in your room, could inspire and stimulate you to go on to bigger and better things.

5

3. Beetle. Canvas applied to wool background. (Mary Mitchell, 11 yrs, Shepperton Green Primary School).

4. Stitch 'doodle' motif of hessian with felt applied in centre. Stitches include couching and french knots. (Girl, 11 yrs).

5. Circular motif using couched threads and cretan stitch. (Jan Beaney).

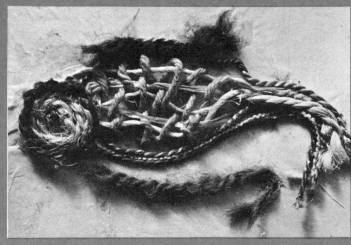

6. Fish—glued and twisted threads; string and wool. (Susan Ward, 10 yrs, Shepperton Green Primary School).

About Embroidery

Embroidery is a pattern, which can be representative or abstract, carried out on material by means of hand or machined stitchery. Sometimes the basic design is built up by applied materials. The majority of historical embroideries show that the stitch technique used to be of prime importance and in many ways this confined the scope of design. Today, embroiderers are going far beyond the old limitations in subjects and materials. As with painting, for some people it is becoming a means of expression.

Embroidery can be used for decorating household articles and dress, or for making pictures, purely as something nice to look at. A scene, an object or part of an object can inspire a design. The main colour, shape or texture of the subject can be over-exaggerated or simplified. Never attempt to imitate painting or the precision of a photograph, as the character of the materials and stitchery should show through in a richness of pattern and colour.

It is very thrilling to create your own individual design. Be adventurous and try to make your own pattern without the aid of transfers. Have a look out of the window for ideas. Perhaps a sprig of leaves outlined against the sky, the pattern between the paving stones of your garden path or the centre of an exotic flower could start you off on your very own design.

Your First Thoughts

First of all, decide what you want to make. Consider its function, size and shape as this dictates the type of materials, threads and stitches you use.

If the article is to be laundered frequently, as a tray cloth would be, for example, washable fabrics and threads such as cotton or linen are best. If you use a variety of materials there is always the possibility of stretching and shrinking which will cause the embroidery to pucker. When making a cushion, choose a strong, firm material suitable for withstanding wear and tear.

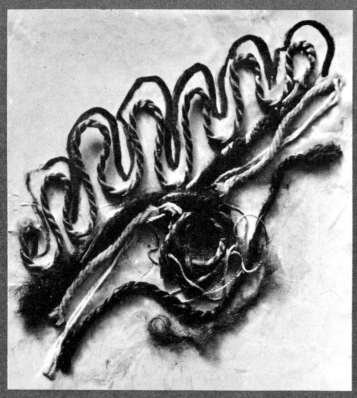

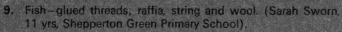

7. Perlita threads and knitting wools glued onto paper to make motif. (Lynne Muir, 10 yrs, Shepperton Green Primary School).

8. Flowers—glued threads. (Helen Green, Shepperton Green Primary School).

9. Fish—glued threads; raffia, string and wool. (Sarah Sworn, 11 yrs, Shepperton Green Primary School).

10. Bird—glued threads. (Sarah Batiste, Shepperton Green Primary School).

The method of embroidery is also an important factor. An article which is to be constantly handled or washed should have fairly close stitchery. Loose stitches will only catch in the iron or your fingers and would become, in time, misshapen.

With purely decorative embroidery such as a picture, there is no need for it to be washed or handled very often. Therefore you can use all sorts of richly coloured and textured materials, threads and stitches. There are no limits and this style of embroidery is most enjoyable to do.

Choosing Threads and Materials

One of the first things you must do is to start your own collection of material and threads. There are a number of interesting mat and shiny threads on the market which vary in thickness. Some are stranded, others are twisted, and they are made in cotton, linen, rayon, silk and wool. Your local shop might only stock one kind of thread so always keep a look out for the embroidery or wool counter of your nearest department store.

There are two important factors to remember. Firstly, choose threads that are in keeping with the material and design. A rug wool would be too heavy for an organdie background and too clumsy for an embroidered device on the pocket of a child's apron. Secondly, do not forget that if your embroidery is decorating an article which is to be washed, choose your threads wisely. Cotton and linen threads, and there are quite a number to choose from, are a safe choice.

Experiment with a few threads. Select two or three, contrasting thick with thin, smooth with rough, shiny with mat. Do not use them all at once as the effect will be spoilt. Arrange a pattern on the table and when you are pleased with it, glue the motif on to a piece of material. Sometimes these attractive 'doodles' make very nice cards.

If you are doing a free decorative panel, there is no limit to the range of threads you may use. You can collect together all types of knitting wools which may be knobbly or crinkly, or a range of slubbed weaving threads if you are lucky enough to live near a handicraft shop. Other exciting yarns can be metal threads, carpet wools, string, raffia and threads drawn from fabrics such as hessian or tweed.

You can easily become confused by the vast choice of materials that you can buy these days. Examples are hessian, linen, slubbed rayón, blistered cloque, shot taffeta, rich velvet, lamé and nets, to name only a few.

When you have decided what fabric will be the most suitable for the particular embroidery planned, decide on a colour scheme. If you are doing free embroidery; for example, a picture or a panel, vary the material by choosing rough, medium and smooth textures within your colour plan.

Look out for materials that you can adapt. Some are loosely woven and look very attractive with threads drawn out or pulled into holes to show other material behind.

Train yourself to be observant and to see new materials and their possibilities. Start a rag bag and make your own collection–you will be amazed at how much you will collect from your friends.

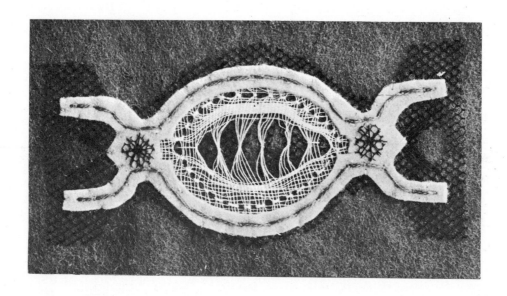

11. Motif–pulled threads. Felt, linen, net applied. (Jan Beaney).

Your Equipment

After you have collected together a variety of materials and threads, you will probably find the following list helpful for the type of embroidery described in this book:

Tape measure

Tacking cotton

Crewel needles in varying sizes, useful for a number of threads:

  chenille (larger eye) – for wool on fairly loose weave materials such as hessian.

  bead (very fine)   – beadwork.

  sharps (fine)   – tacking; for making up articles.

Thimble

Tailors' chalk for marking patterns on material.

Pins

Scissors

Stiletto – useful for making holes in fabric to ease through thick threads when couching.

Frame – tambour (round). Helpful for when you want to work on material which is taut as in beadwork.

Paints, brushes, pencils and paper for designing.

Tracing paper.

12. Equipment.

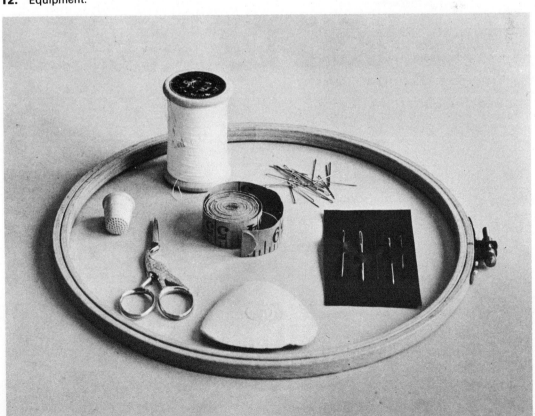

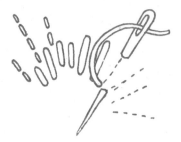

STRAIGHT STITCH This is shown as single spaced stitches worked either in a regular or irregular manner. Sometimes the stitches are of varying size.

COUCHING Lay a thread along line of design and with another thread tie it down at even intervals with a small stitch into the fabric.

CHAIN STITCH Bring thread out at top of line and hold down with left thumb. Insert needle where it last emerged and bring point out a short distance away. Pull thread through keeping working thread under needle point.
DETACHED CHAIN STITCH Work in the same way as chain stitch but fasten each loop at the foot with a small stitch.

SEEDING This simple filling stitch is composed of small straight stitches of equal length placed at random over the surface as shown on the diagram.

Some Useful Stitches

Try some simple experiments, just to gain experience and not for any particular purpose. As you can see by looking at the illustrations, you can make quite a good effect with a few simple stitches. Couching is the first line stitch and is useful for laying the foundation of any embroidery.

Select a piece of material, needle and thread and try some of the stitches shown on the next few pages. When you think you have mastered some of them, make up a small motif of lines and simple shapes combining two or three stitches. Remember to fasten on and off securely with a double stitch on the wrong side of your work.

Never make the mistake of thinking you need to use lots of stitches for creating a successful embroidery. A few well-chosen stitches can make a rich decoration without its being overcrowded.

TWISTED CHAIN STITCH Commence as for chain stitch but instead of inserting needle into the place from which it emerged, insert it close to last loop and take small slanting stitch coming out on line of design. Pull thread through. Work loops close together.

12

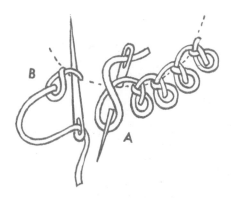

PEKINESE STITCH Work back stitch and interlace with thread.

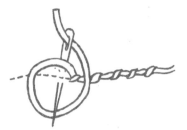

CORAL STITCH Bring thread out at right end of line, lay thread along line of design and hold down with left thumb. Take a small stitch under the line and thread, and pull through bringing needle over lower thread.

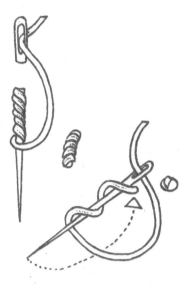

BULLION KNOTS Pick up a back stitch the size of knot required bringing needle point out where it first emerged; do not pull right through fabric. Twist thread round needle point as many times as required to equal space of back stitch. Hold left thumb on coiled thread and pull needle through. Turn needle back and insert again at place where it was first inserted. Pull thread through until knot lies flat.

FRENCH KNOTS Bring thread through. Hold thread down with left thumb and encircle thread twice with needle. Still holding thread, twist needle back to starting point and insert close to where thread first emerged. Pull thread through to back and secure or pass to next knot.

ROSETTE CHAIN STITCH Bring thread through at right end of upper line, pass across to left side and hold down with left thumb. Insert needle into upper line a short distance from where the thread emerged and bring it out just above the lower line, passing thread under needle point (A). Draw needle through and pass under top thread without picking up any fabric (B).

13. Circular motif. Stitches include chain stitch, pekinese stitch, couching and french knots. (Janet Holliday, 5th form, Eliots Green Grammar School).

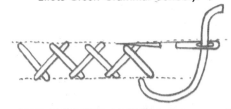

HERRINGBONE STITCH Bring needle out on lower line at left side and insert on upper line a little to the right taking small stitch to left with thread below needle. Next insert needle on lower line a little to the right and take small stitch to the left with thread above needle. Work these two movements alternately.

13

14. Circular motif inspired by an ancient medallion; worked in carpet wool offcuts on hessian. (Jan Beaney).

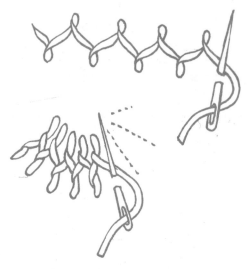

CRETAN STITCH Working from the left bring thread through between upper and lower lines. Insert needle at lower line and make small vertical stitch towards upper line keeping thread to right of needle. Next, insert needle on upper line and make small vertical stitch towards lower line keeping wool to right of needle.

SHEAF STITCH Work three straight stitches and hold down with two horizontal stitches.

FISHBONE STITCH Bring thread through and make small straight stitch along the centre line of the shape. Bring thread through to right of first stitch. Make a sloping stitch across centre line at base of first stitch. Bring thread through on left side and make a similar sloping stitch to overlap the previous stitch.

15. Motif. Surface stitchery and beadwork. (Susan Plank, 4th form, Eliots Green Grammar School).

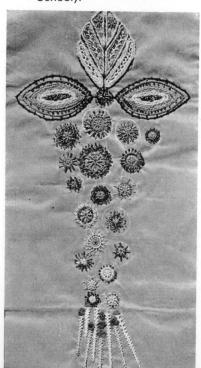

DOUBLE KNOT STITCH Bring thread through and take small stitch across guide line. Pass needle downwards under surface stitch just made without piercing fabric. With thread under needle pass needle again under first stitch and pull thread through to form a knot. Knots should be spaced evenly and closely to obtain a beading effect.

14

RAISED CHAIN BAND Work required number of foundation bars which are fairly closely spaced horizontal straight stitches. Bring thread through to the top then pass needle upwards under centre of first bar and to the left. With thread under needle, pass needle downwards to the right and pull up the chain loop thus formed.

BRICK STITCH Worked in blocks of horizontal and vertical straight stitches.

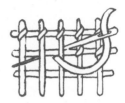

COUCHED FILLING consists of long evenly spaced stitches taken across the space horizontally and vertically. Then crossed threads are tied down at all intersecting points.

Some of your more successful stitch 'doodles' will make attractive cards and you could always enrich a motif with a few small beads clustered in the middle or around one of the shapes. Never overdo the beading, and select colours that tone in with the main scheme. Contrasting coloured beads and sequins can spoil the look of your work.

For sewing down beads, use a bead needle and a fine but strong thread such as silk. Sequins look at their best if held in place by a small bead, the method being to pass the thread through the material, sequin and bead and back through the sequin and cloth and on to the next one. The texture and filling stitches illustrated on this page will help to enrich your design once you have embroidered in the line stitches as the framework of your pattern.

FEATHER STITCH Bring needle out at top centre, hold thread down with left thumb, insert needle a little to right on same level and take small stitch down to centre keeping thread under needle point. Insert needle a little to left on same level and take stitch to centre keeping thread under needle point. Work these two movements alternately.

BACKSTITCH WHEEL Work eight straight stitches into the centre (a). Bring thread through to the middle and then over and under the stitch behind and on to the next one (b). Repeat until required effect is obtained (c). Fasten off by taking thread over the stitch behind and through to back of material.

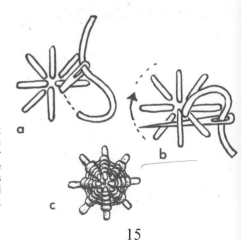

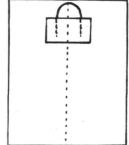

16

17

16. Greetings card. Upholstery fabric with felt centre. Knots, cretan stitch and straight stitch are among those used. (Jan Beaney).
17. How to make your calendar.

Making a Greetings Card and a Calendar

You will need a piece of card or stiff paper. If you haven't any at home it can be bought from a stationer's shop or an artists' materials suppliers.

Cut it to the size you require and fold carefully in half. Cut out your embroidered motif from the remaining material taking care not to cut too close to the stitches. Trim the ends at the back.

Paste a glue, such as Copydex, which is suitable for sticking material, evenly over the back. Do not put so much on that it soaks through to the front spoiling the work. Place on the front of the card. The space between the motif and the edge of the card should be very slightly larger at the bottom.

To make a calendar you would need one piece of stiff card, a short length of ribbon and a small calendar. Glue the embroidered motif and calendar carefully in place as described above. Loop the ribbon on the top edge of the card and neatly secure the ends on the wrong side with a small piece of gummed paper (Fig. 17).

How to Begin Designing

Having determined the method and material of your embroidery, the design is the next stage. If you keep a sketchbook and a collection of magazine and newspaper cuttings and photographs for reference you will probably have lots of ideas.

There are three main points to remember. Choose a subject or pattern that will be fitting for the purpose of the embroidery. For example, a picture designed for a nursery would not always be suitable for a dining-room.

The second point is, make the design fit the shape of the article to be embroidered.

Thirdly, consider whether the colour scheme is suitable for the particular function of the article.

18. Detail from wall hanging. Tapestry with stitches overlaid. (Humble Oil Refinery, Texas).
19. 'Madonna' Christmas card. Machine embroidery on rep. (Audrey Tucker, 1962 Group).

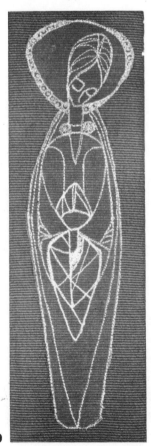

18   19

20

20. Sketch for embroidery illustrating how a pleasing shape can be made of a bird in a nest.
21. Panel—'Half Melon'. Applied nets, hand and machine embroidery. Twisted chain stitch and beads add to the effect. (Kathleen Petyt, 1962 Group).
22. Detail—skirt border, Crete 1733. Notice how the repeating patterns vary in size and shape. (Victoria and Albert Museum, Crown Copyright).

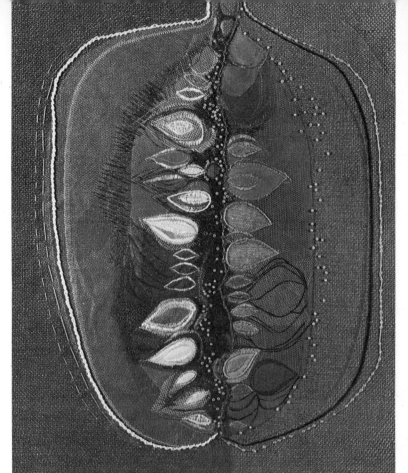

21

 22

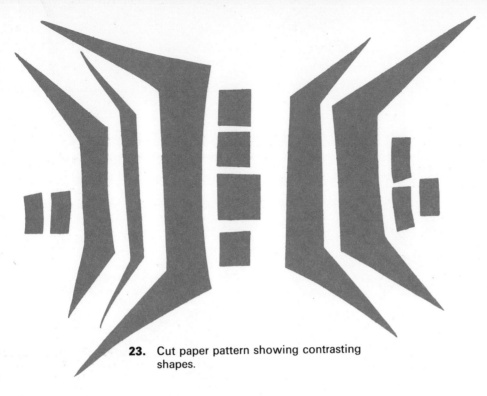

23. Cut paper pattern showing contrasting shapes.

The Importance of Shapes

Allow the design room to expand as the idea develops. Do not take the design to the edge of the material or let the pattern 'grow' from the side. In most cases keep the design compact within the shape.

Remember to keep the interest in the picture: have a focal point. Everything else in the design should help to emphasize this point, and planning the background spaces is essential.

Have big shapes and helping shapes if the motif is to be repeated. Forms of the same size can be boring. Contrasting lines with solid shapes can also help to make a pleasing pattern.

24. Sketch for embroidery design—Sea Urchin; West Indies.

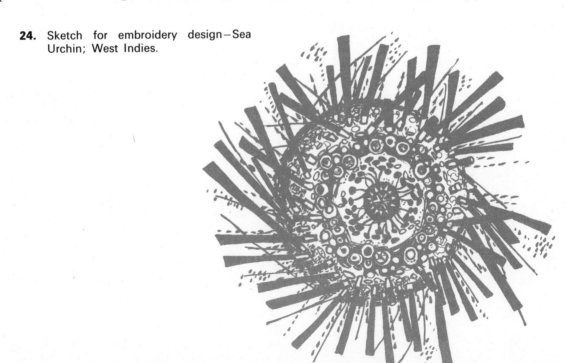

Make a drawing of a flower and notice the intricate patterns and markings. Simplify these points into a design. Observe how the flower designs illustrated in this book are contrived into certain shapes and how charming they are. The Elizabethans were especially fond of floral devices and embroidered them on many things.

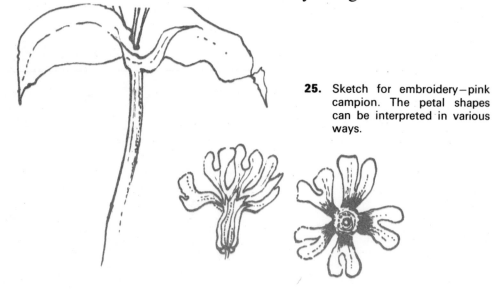

25. Sketch for embroidery—pink campion. The petal shapes can be interpreted in various ways.

Choosing Your Colour Scheme

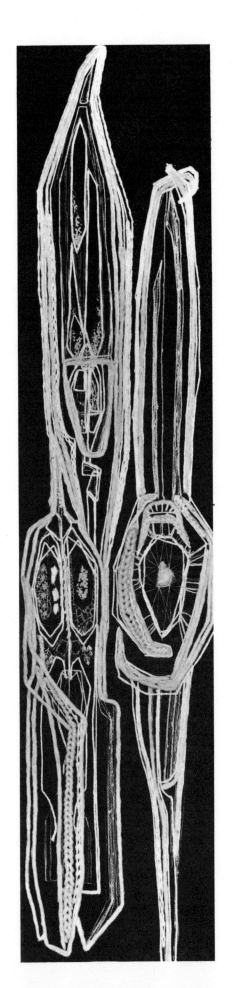

Always keep a look out for ideas for colour schemes. There are many beautiful colour plans all round you in everyday life. If you look at a vast scene you will be overwhelmed by so many colours that you will not know where to start. Take a close and long look at a detail of that scene. You can collect a lifetime of schemes by training yourself to observe such things as speckling on the back of a toadstool, rain-sodden tree trunks, fading leaves in autumn, subtle-coloured fish scales, wet paving stones or slate tiles, pebbles on a beach, the inside of an oyster shell, oil in a puddle; the list is endless.

However, there are a few safe rules to re-member. Never use every colour you can think of in one design. The colour should suit the function of the embroidery. Choose a main colour and then add smaller amounts of helping or complimentary colours in light and dark shades. Some embroideries that are carried out in one colour but in varying tones, are often most successful.

26. 'Snowdrops'—panel. Machine and hand stitchery. (Audrey Tucker, 1962 Group).

27. Bird appliqué. (Sarah Batiste, Shepperton Green Primary School).

28. 'Pagoda'—panel. Applied fabrics on rep. (4th form, Eliots Green Grammar School).

29. Moth Appliqué. Applied felt, net and other materials. (Gillian Hodgson).

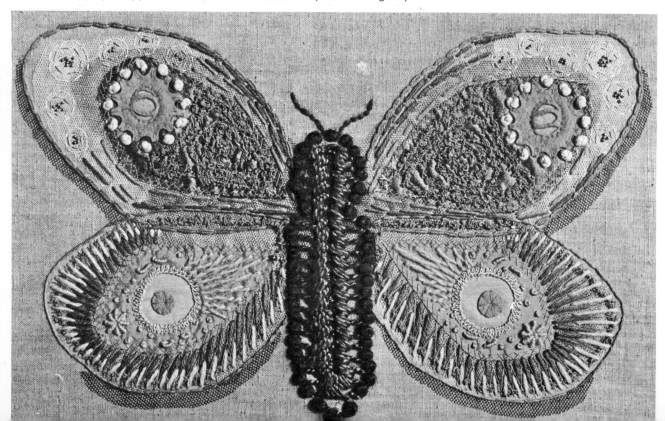

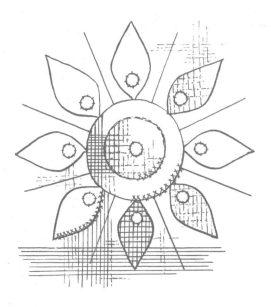

30

30. How to match warp and weft.
31. The rule of matching warp to weft has been broken here to obtain the feathery back and tail of the seagull. However, it is wise to keep to the rule unless you need a special effect which can only be gained by deliberately not matching them.

31

Appliqué

Appliqué is the term used for the technique of applying one material on to a background fabric and enriching with stitchery.

If you are making a decorative picture or a motif for a cushion cover using applied pieces of fabric, work out carefully where they are to be placed before sewing down. You can either transfer the design from paper to fabric as described on page 44 or you can draw freely on the material with a white pencil or tailors' chalk if you feel confident enough.

Always remember when applying material to match the way the threads run (the warp and weft as it is called) of both the material to be applied and the background, to prevent puckering (Fig. 30).

All fabric should be herringbone stitched to the ground material to stop the edges fraying. Net and felt do not fray and can be stitched around the edge with small catch stitches. All stitching should be done in a fine thread with a colour to match the material.

Why not attempt a small appliqué motif?

a

Making an Appliqué Panel

Cut out in paper a simple shape, perhaps a bird or a flower.

The design you have cut out can be used as a pattern for the material you wish to apply. Remember to match the grain of the fabric.

Choose interesting fabrics such as a smooth material to be applied to a textured one. Keep to a simple colour scheme.

Pin the pieces on to the background material, tack and sew down as described (Fig. 32a).

Develop the main design with line stitches. Sometimes follow the edges of the applied pieces and other times break into the background spaces (Fig. 32b).

Enrich some areas with textured stitchery (Fig. 32c).

Emphasize the focal point by using a certain stitch, a spot of intense colour or a change in tone or texture. The motif shown on these pages is worked in wool and cotton but the focal point is made important by the use of a shiny thread, slightly lighter in tone and speckled with tiny beads (Fig. 33).

b

c

32. *a, b, c.* Making appliqué panel—'Bird in Nest'.

33. Appliqué panel complete. (Jan Beaney).

34. Detail from an embroidered picture 'David and Bathsheba', showing how padding was used in the 17th century when it was called 'stumpwork'. English 1656. (Victoria and Albert Museum, Crown Copyright).

Padding

Padding is fun to do and can enrich some designs for free embroidery. The historical example illustrated was done in the 17th century when the padding often consisted of small blocks of wood covered with white satin. The method explained here is quite simple and the pad is made of felt.

When you have decided on the size and shape of the intended raised part, cut a piece of felt exactly to the size. Follow with two or three other pieces each the same shape but slightly smaller than the one before (Fig. 35a). The more layers of felt you use, the more raised the padding will be (Fig. 35b). Tack the pieces together. Cut out the covering material, the same shape but about a $\frac{1}{4}''$ larger all round. Work a small running stitch around the edge (Fig. 35c). Place the felt filling in the centre of the material and pull the thread tightly so that the material curls itself round the felt. Secure the thread (Fig. 35d). Apply the pad to the background material by small hem stitches, taking care to tuck in any surplus material as you go (Fig. 35e).

35. *a, b, c, d, e.* Method of padding.

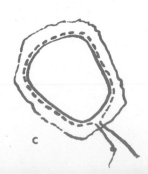

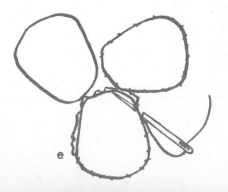

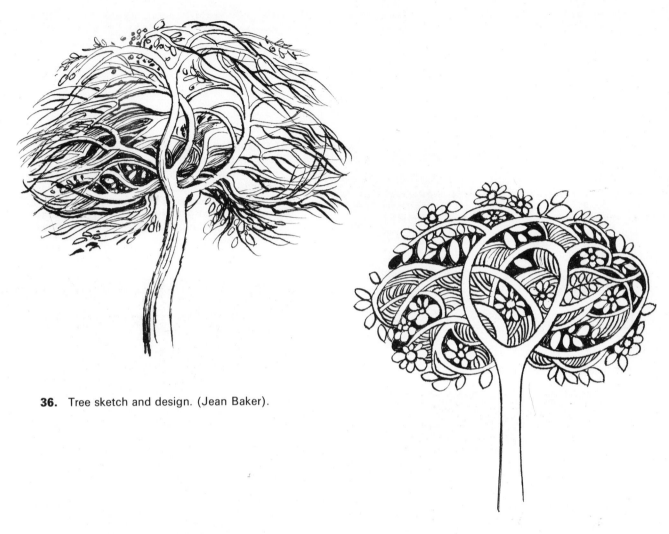

36. Tree sketch and design. (Jean Baker).

Keeping a Sketchbook

Endeavour to cultivate the habit of keeping a sketchbook as it can be the source of many pleasing designs. Take notice of anything that catches your eye whether it is a scene, a peculiar shape of tree, a group of pebbles on a beach or the pattern of sweets in a jar.

Do not become too disheartened if your sketches are not easily recognizable at first. You will improve with regular practice. When beginning a sketch, always take note of the proportions of one thing to another and the shape and size of the spaces between the objects. First draw a rough sketch remembering these points and then add details and an indication of textures.

When you have collected some examples look carefully at your subjects. Pick out one you like and consider it in terms of pattern, material and stitches as described on pages 7 and 8.

Simplify or emphasize any parts you wish.

27

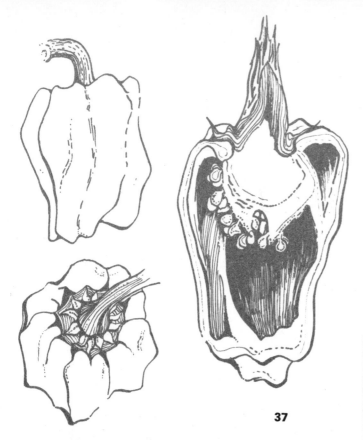

37

37. Sketches, Green Peppers.
38. Panel—'Cross-Section of a Pepper'. Hand and machine embroidery, some beadwork; net, felt, silk applied. The spaces have been emphasized. (Jan Beaney).
39. Panel—'Sun Caught in Tree'. Hand and machine embroidery. (Jean Carter, 1962 Group).

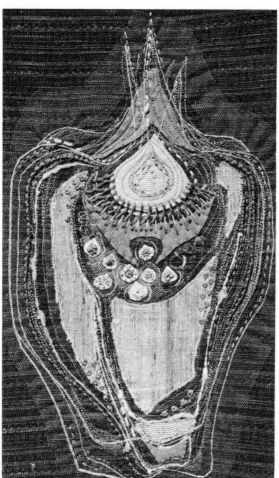

38

39

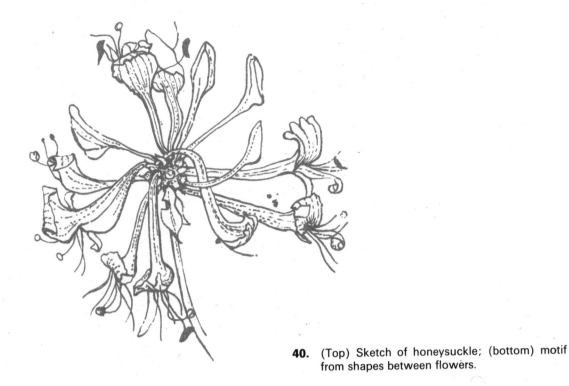

40. (Top) Sketch of honeysuckle; (bottom) motif from shapes between flowers.

The design on this page has been made from the sketch of a plant. The spaces between the stems and flowers make the pattern, not the flower itself. This fascinating pattern could look most pleasing embroidered on the end of a tray cloth or cushion if placed correctly.

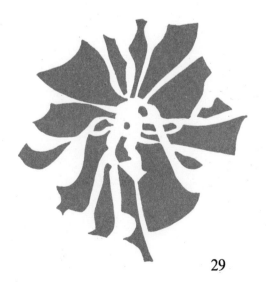

41

41. Design—adapted from eagle taken from Egyptian panel.
42. Jewel box. Small pieces of felt applied to tie silk. Some double knot stitch, french knots and beadwork. (Jan Beaney).
43. Detail from bedspread. American 1770. (The Metropolitan Museum of Art. Rogers Fund 1922).

42

43

44. Detail of Syon Cope. English, late 13th century. Silk and silver-gilt threads. (Victoria and Albert Museum. Crown Copyright).
45. Detail of skirt border. Crete 18th century. Linen embroidery with silk in cretan, feather and herringbone stitches among others. (Victoria and Albert Museum, Crown Copyright).

Going to Museums

44

You can gather together many exciting designs by visiting and sketching in a museum. When looking at natural forms or patterns from the work of craftsmen of the past you will find a wealth of ideas.

Having discovered something you like, perhaps from a vase or a pendant, copy the basic character of the pattern. When using the motif in an embroidery you can make colour and texture variations or emphasize one part more than another.

Your ideas might develop into a repeat pattern for bead embroidery on an evening stole or a casket, or a decorative device for a cushion. The possibilities are endless.

45

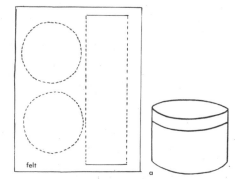

Making a Paperweight —Inspired by a Museum Motif

46. *a, b, c.* Making a paperweight.

Your first aim is to find an object which is heavy enough for a paper weight.

A straight sided, circular cosmetic jar filled with sand or a piece of steel would be suitable.

Cut a strip of felt to fit closely around the weight and two circular pieces for the top and base (Fig. 46a).

Work the embroidered motif on the top material before making up. An elaborate top and plain sides is most practicable for handling.

Using a matching thread, oversew the ends of the strip of material together as neatly as possible (Fig. 46b). Stitch the top material in position, insert the weight and sew on the bottom piece (Fig. 46c).

Having made sure all is secure, you can neaten the top seam with a couched thread.

47. Finished paperweight, with couched braiding, knots and cretan stitch. (Jan Beaney).

48. Panel—'Lion'. A fine example of a backstitch wheel can be seen under his tail. (Diane Musson, 4th year, Eliots Green Grammar School).

A Visit to the Zoo

There are many exciting subjects to be seen at the zoo—lions and tigers, owls and flamingos, angel fish and turtles and so many other creatures.

49

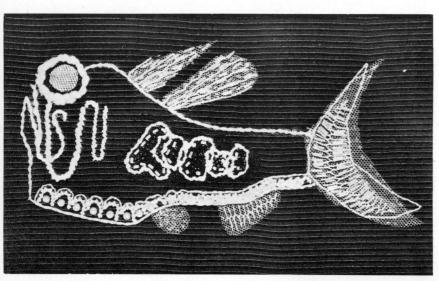

50

49. Design for embroidery —
tiger. (Janet Bedford,
4th year, Eliots Green
Grammar School).

50. 'White Fish'. (Pat Wilson,
lower 6th, Eliots Green
Grammar School).

51. Elephant — detail from
border. Chinese. (Em-
broiderers' Guild Collec-
tion).

51

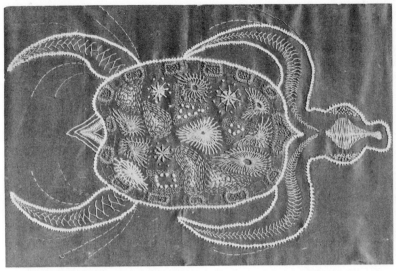

If you take photographs or make drawings of any of them, look and see if they are marked in such a way that you can make the pattern much bolder when turning the subject into an embroidery design. If you look at the photographs in this section you will see how other people have interpreted this. The rough patchy skin of a rhinoceros is shown by applying buttons, beads and pieces of wood. The shell of the tortoise is exaggerated by stitch patterns and the lion's mane is represented by felt pieces. You can still recognize the creature's identity but they have been made to look more decorative.

Why not choose an animal or bird that you like and carry out a small appliqué picture for your room?

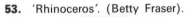

53. 'Rhinoceros'. (Betty Fraser).

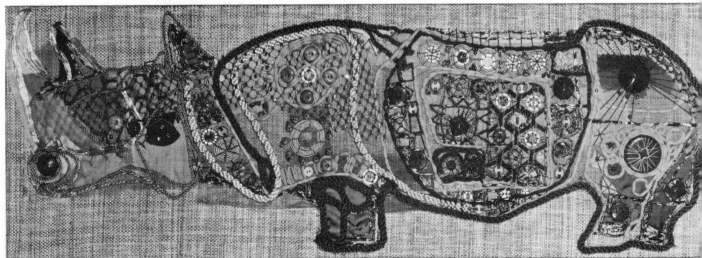

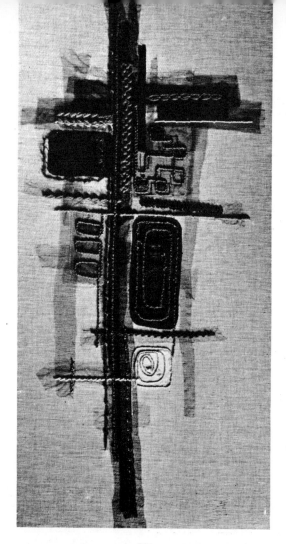

54. Panel. Applied nets and couching on curtain material. Raised chain bands predominate. (Janet Thorpe, Whitelands College).

55. Cut paper pattern.

56. Cut paper patterns.

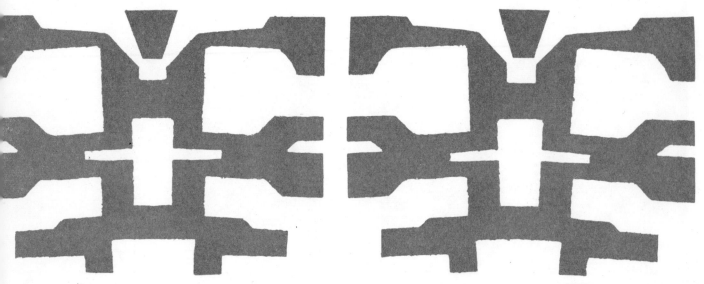

Cut Paper Patterns

Cut paper patterns are original and are great fun to do. Find some scrap paper and a pair of paper-cutting scissors and start by cutting out different shapes.

You can fold the paper several times, cut out some shapes and when you open the paper you will find some sort of pattern. If you are not pleased with it, fold it again and cut out some more pieces. Always remember to cut out big pieces and little pieces, as one contrasts with the other.

Another method is to cut out separate pieces and to place one next to the other with small spaces between as shown on this page. Keep to simple shapes and make the background spaces as interesting as the actual paper pieces.

Once the desired pattern is obtained, it is then cut out again in cloth and applied to the background material. Remember to match the warp and weft of both fabrics. You can also pin the paper patterns to the ground material and chalk or tack round the shapes. Having tacked the outline of the design, you can embroider in and around the motif.

The design on the opposite page originated from a cut paper pattern.

37

57. Paper pattern cut out in separate pieces.

A Decorative Fingerplate

Buy yourself one of the plastic or glass fingerplate panels used for preventing fingermarks on doors. Choose fairly fine materials and threads and a certain colour scheme.

To enable you to determine the size and shape of the embroidery, cut a sheet of paper to the exact size of the fingerplate. Fold it and cut out a pattern as described on the previous page. Use the cut-out as the basis of your design. Sew down any materials as suggested on page 23. Try and contrive the screwholes into the design.

Carry out the embroidery using fairly flat stitches so that the glass panel can be fitted closely to the work. Having completed the motif, stretch and mount over card as described on page 48. Enclose behind the glass panel and screw carefully to the door.

58. *A,* and *B.* Making a fingerplate:
    (A1) the cut paper pattern
    (B2) apply pieces of material
    (B3) enrich with stitchery.

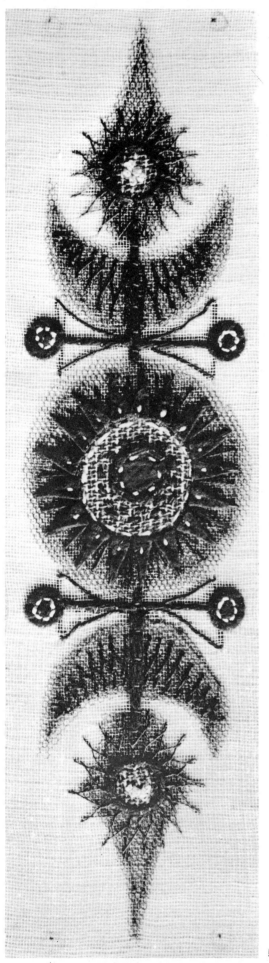

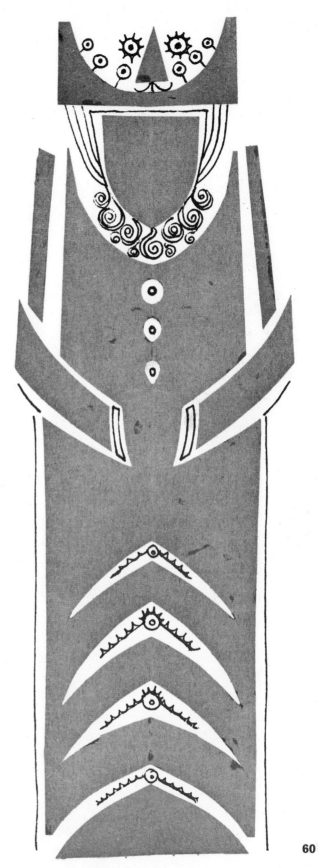

59. Completed fingerplate panel. (Jan Beaney).
60. A cut paper pattern with drawn details.

59

Taking Rubbings

Some people find it very difficult to make abstract designs which are interesting in shape and texture. By taking rubbings from different surfaces, you will collect a wide selection of patterns to choose from. Of course you have to pick out the most interesting part and decide whether it will suit the particular shape of the article to be embroidered. Usually the rubbings vary in tone so you can pick your threads accordingly. The thickness of line can be interpreted by line stitches in a variety of threads.

For making a rubbing you need some thin paper and a black greasy crayon or 2B pencil. Place the paper over a surface, perhaps a rough bark of a tree, holding firmly in place and shade across in one direction. Do not press too hard as the pencil will pierce the paper, nor too lightly as little or no impression will be made.

On collecting some patterns, look carefully at all the shapes and select a part you like. Always look for a main shape or focal point and helping shapes. If the pattern is too small for what you want, copy the design in a larger scale on to another sheet of paper.

61. Rubbings. *a,* shell; *b,* shell; *c,* stone; *d,* slate; *e,* base of wickerbasket.

62. Detail from embroidered panel of beach tunic inspired by bark rubbings. (Gillian Bragg, Whitelands Training College).

63. Drawing of the beach tunic. (Gillian Bragg).

When you find you have a particularly pleasing design, copy the main features of it on to your material with a white pencil or tailors' chalk and embroider.

An applied decoration inspired by a rubbing could look nice on a cushion or for a dress embroidery. The sample shown is a detail from a front panel of a towelling beach tunic.

64. Rubbing—tree bark.
65. Tree bark—showing interesting patterns.

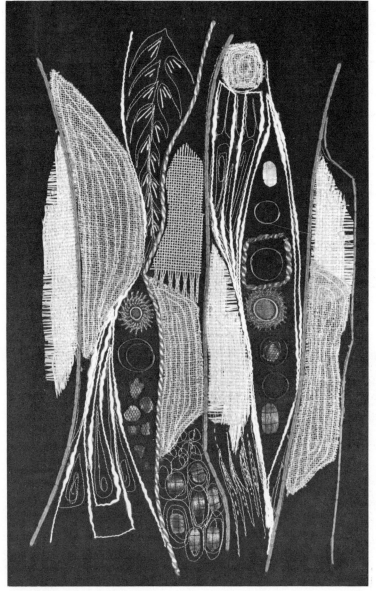

66

66. Cross section of stem. Applied work. Couched threads, wood shavings and stones held down by net. (Jan Beaney).
67. Design—cell structure.
68. Cell structure. Stitchery on hessian. (Barbara Priest, lower 6th, Eliots Green Grammar School).

68

67

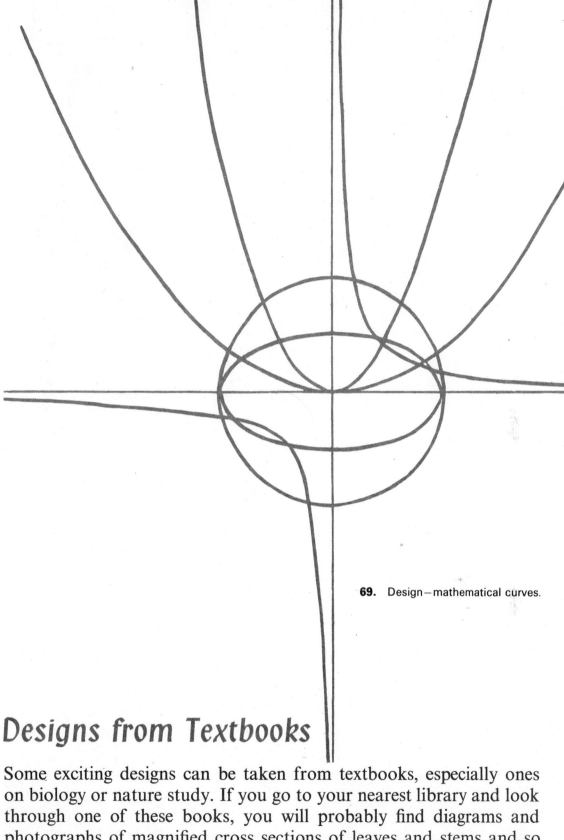

69. Design—mathematical curves.

Designs from Textbooks

Some exciting designs can be taken from textbooks, especially ones on biology or nature study. If you go to your nearest library and look through one of these books, you will probably find diagrams and photographs of magnified cross sections of leaves and stems and so on. Some of the patterns are very exciting and if used as embroidery designs in good colour and with a variety of interesting threads, they can be fun to do.

43

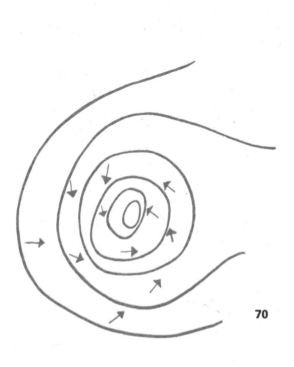

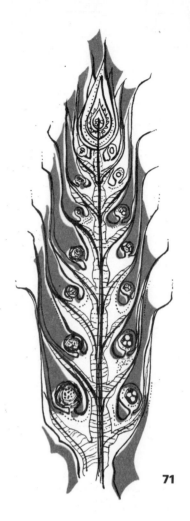

70. Design—cyclonic depression out of context.
71. Sketch—selaginella section.

Once you have found a pattern you like, you need only take a part of
the cross section (the part that has the nicest shapes in your opinion)
and draw it much larger on to a piece of thin paper—taking care to
show the main character of the shapes and the spaces between the
shapes. These are very important.

Choose an interesting piece of material for the background and tack
your piece of paper firmly on to it tacking also around the main lines
of your design. Make sure that you fasten on and off securely.

When this is completed, very gently tear away the paper and the tacking stitches in the drawn design will be left on your material. Having
already selected a colour scheme, you can then apply pieces of
material in certain parts and contrast with line and filling stitches
in varying types of thread in some of the remaining shapes.

Never overcrowd the design with too much material or too many
stitches. Leave some empty spaces to contrast with others.

44

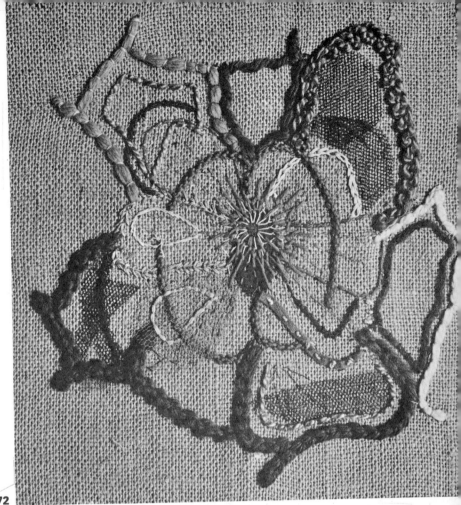

72. Cell structure. Applied felt and nets on hessian background enriched with stitchery. (Pat Wilson, lower 6th, Eliots Green Grammar School).

73. Cross section II. Linen, net and stitchery applied to hessian. (Jan Beaney).

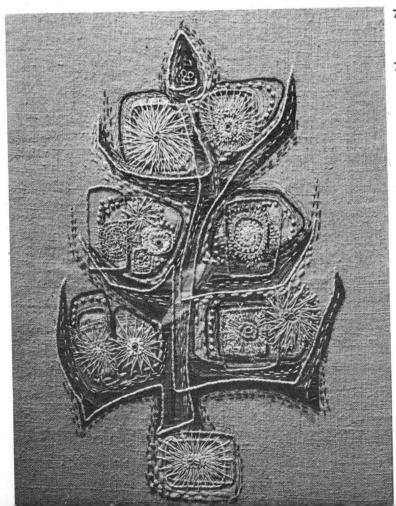

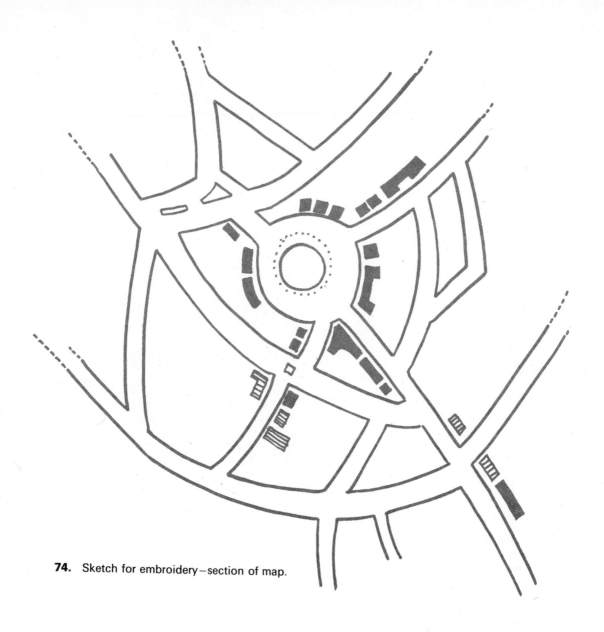

74. Sketch for embroidery—section of map.

Map Patterns

Attractive, original designs spring from many sources. The pattern on this page developed from parts of a town map taken out of its context. The same principle of choosing a focal point was observed and the pattern was greatly simplified. Obviously a section of map would have to be carefully chosen and its chief characteristics highlighted before it would be suitable for an embroidered motif—as with any idea in its first stage.

Making a Cushion

When designing for a cushion it is advisable to make the pattern
   attractive from all angles.

Remember to use suitable fabrics and stitchery.

Having decided on the size of the cushion, carefully cut out matching
   sides allowing for half-inch turnings.

Transfer the design and carry out the embroidery.

Place the right sides of the cushion cover together, tack and machine
   or back-stitch three sides (Fig. 75a).

Turn the cover right side out and press.

Cut out a lining case about an inch smaller all round than your
   cushion cover. Sew together on three sides. Turn inside out and
   stuff with a suitable filling such as foam rubber or kapok. Sew along
   the top so that the filling is entirely enclosed.

Insert into the cover and slip stitch neatly along the remaining side
   (Fig. 75b).

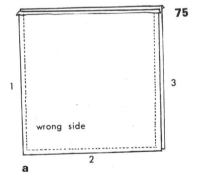

75

wrong side

a

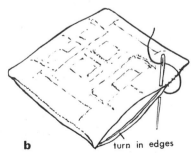

b   turn in edges

75. *a,* and *b.* Making a cushion.
76. Finished cushion. (Christine Nuth, Whitelands College).

76

Stretching and Mounting

Most embroideries, especially panels, need to be stretched on completion. All the creases will be removed without the stitchery being flattened as it would be if it was ironed.

You will need a drawing board, drawing pins and two or three layers of blotting paper.

Wet the blotting paper and stretch it flat on the board. Place the embroidery wrong side downwards and pin along one side. Repeat the process on the remaining sides pulling the material quite tautly. Make sure that the weave is kept straight in both directions (Fig. 77).

Having stretched your work you will need to mount it if it is going to be a picture. The materials needed are strawboard or card, a needle and some tough thread such as button or carpet thread. Use the firmer strawboard if your panel is quite large. Thinner card will do for smaller pieces.

Cut the board to the correct size. Place the embroidery right side downwards on a table and the board on top in the right position. Fold the edges over and pin temporarily in place.

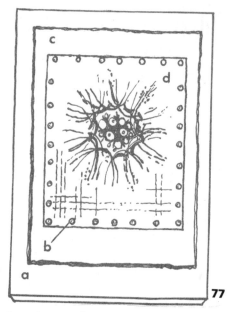

77.

77. Method of stretching, *a*, drawing board; *b* and *c*, blotting paper; *d*, embroidery. Pin round, keeping warp and weft straight.

78. Method of mounting. *a*, lace from side to side, middle to outer edge; *b*, lace from top to bottom, middle to outer edge.

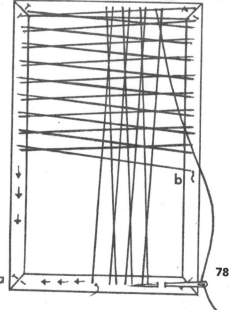

78

Fasten the thread securely in the centre of one side and then commence lacing from side to side pulling the thread tightly and working from middle to outer edge of each side. Remember to fasten on and off securely each time you need to renew the thread (Fig. 78).

The panel can now be easily framed.

48

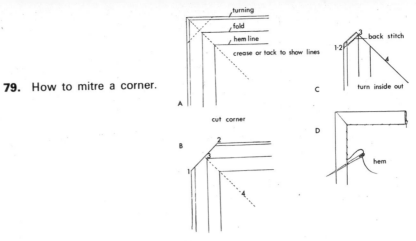

79. How to mitre a corner.

Other Points to Remember

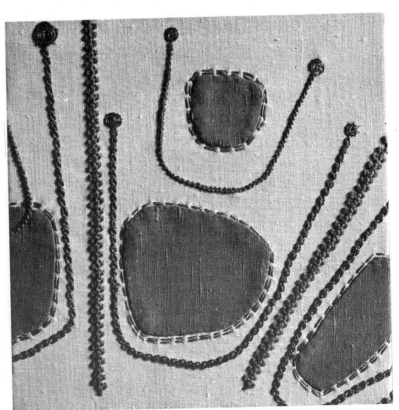

80. Detail from tablecloth. (Erian Short, Embroiderers' Guild Collection).

Embroidery Yesterday—Today

It is always interesting to see examples of historical and present day embroidery in the various fields of the craft. You will probably like, and be encouraged by, some aspect of both. Perhaps you can work out from where the embroiderers evolved their ideas. Notice the type of threads, stitches and material used to give certain effects.

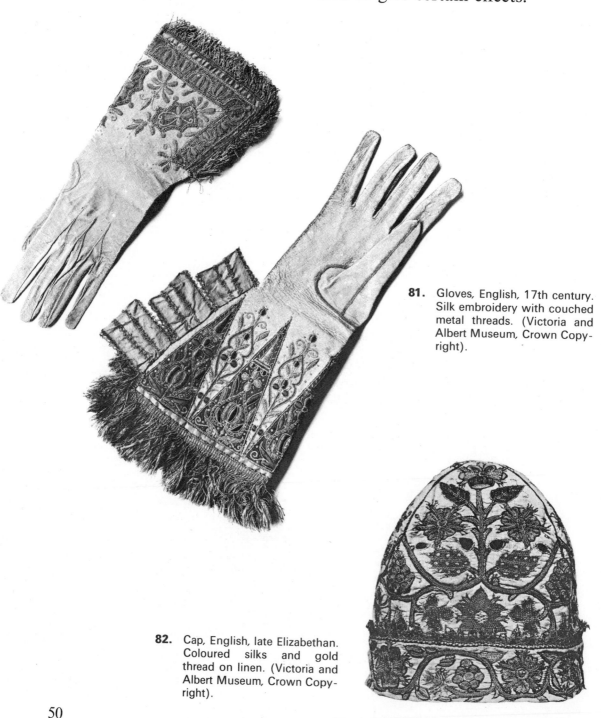

81. Gloves, English, 17th century. Silk embroidery with couched metal threads. (Victoria and Albert Museum, Crown Copyright).

82. Cap, English, late Elizabethan. Coloured silks and gold thread on linen. (Victoria and Albert Museum, Crown Copyright).

84

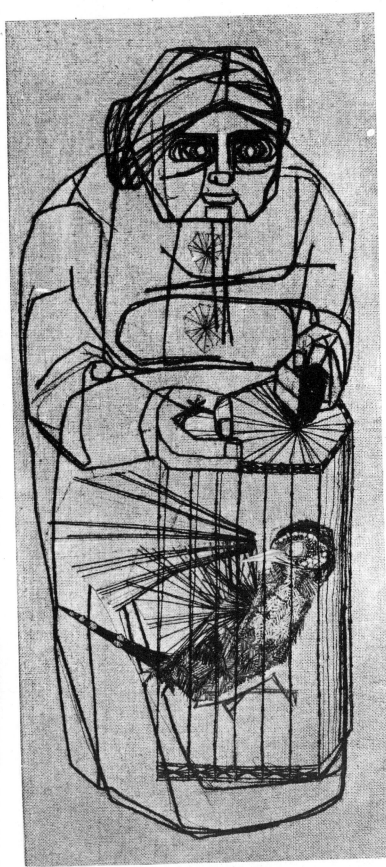

83. Panel—'Old Woman and Bird'. Hand and machine embroidery. (Audrey Tucker, 1962 Group).
84. Bird—detail from border. Chinese. (Embroiderers' Guild Collection).
85. Detail from panel. Interesting threads. (June Tiley, 1962 Group).

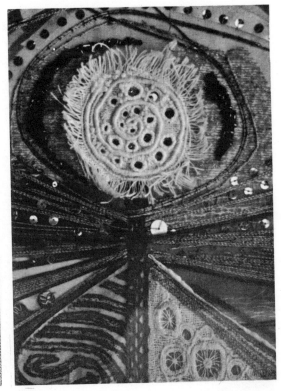

83

85

86. Man's jacket. Hungarian, 19th century. Sheepskin with applied ornaments in coloured leather. (Victoria and Albert Museum, Crown Copyright).

87. Sketch for embroidered evening stole. (Barbara Priest, Eliots Green Grammar School).

88. Panel—'Robin in a Snow-storm'. Hand and machine embroidery. (Jean Carter, 1962 Group).

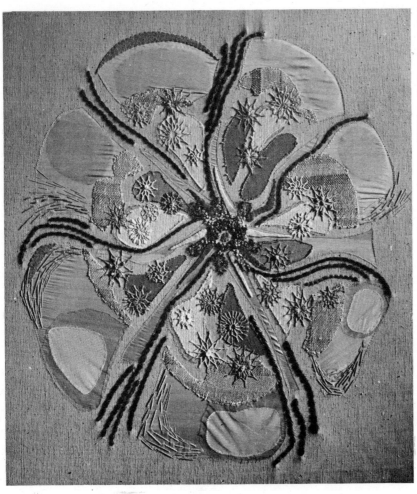

89. 'Flower'. Appliqué, with couching, straight stitch, french knots and cretan stitch. (Gillian Cook, Whitelands College).

Within the tight limitation of church embroidery, some very stimulating work is being done with rich and unusual materials: the designs seem less stiff and formal.

Embroidery on dress is also very exciting. The trend is more for an interesting all-over texture to give a subtle richness to the outfit rather than contrasting colours and isolated motifs. Machine embroidery is becoming increasingly popular on undergarments, childrens' clothes and evening wear. There is a high degree of skill needed for machine embroidery to be wholly successful. However, once mastered, it is a fairly quick method of working and it suits the pace of living today. You will probably find it great fun to do if you ever have the chance to use the right sort of machine. There are a few books listed on page 57 which will help you to make a start in this method of embroidery.

90. Detail from cushion. English, late 16th century. Silver-gilt and silver threads, metal strip and silk in straight stitch and couching. (Victoria and Albert Museum, Crown Copyright).

91. Detail of whitework skirt border of muslin dress. English, 19th century. Cotton thread, drawn thread work filled in with needlepoint stitches. (Victoria and Albert Museum, Crown Copyright).

92. Panel—'Minerva'. (Jean Baker).

Free embroidery today is being accepted much more as an art form. Educational authorities and private collectors are including embroidered panels in their collections. Professional artists are commissioned to work panels and hangings for decorating private apartments and public buildings. Two examples are shown on this page. One is a detail taken from a ninety-two foot wall-hanging for a cafeteria in an oil refinery in Texas. The other panel is to hang in the board room of a large firm in Southampton.

93. One of 14 wall panels. John Smith Cafeteria, Humble Oil Company, Texas.

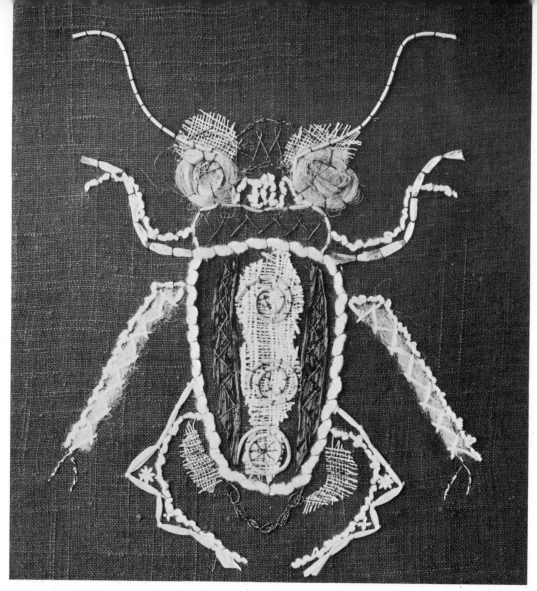

94. 'Beetle'. Wool, string, thin cane and raffia on linen. (Maureen Southey, Whitelands College).

Conclusion

When you design for, or work, embroidery, try to keep an open mind. Do not think of the craft just as the execution of neat stitchery. Combine all the aspects of the craft that you have learnt from this book. Drawing, pattern making and the choice of fabric, colour, threads and suitable stitchery, all have their part to play in a successful piece of work. Always remember to consider carefully the function of whatever you are making and whether the design and method of embroidery are appropriate.

The scope of embroidery is immense and the joy is that you can work at home and the amount of equipment needed is small compared to some crafts.

The most important point of all, is to enjoy yourself in whatever aspect of the craft you choose to do.

Other Books about Embroidery

CREATIVE TEXTILE CRAFT: THREAD AND FABRIC
By Rolf Hartung: U.K., Batsford, 1964; U.S.A., Reinholdt, 1964

DICTIONARY OF EMBROIDERY STITCHES
By Mary Thomas: U.K., Hodder & Stoughton, 13th imp. 1956;
U.S.A., Morrow, 1935

EMBROIDERY—A FRESH APPROACH
By Alison Liley: U.K., Mills & Boon, 1964; U.S.A., Taplinger, 1964

ENGLISH HISTORICAL EMBROIDERY
By Barbara Snook: U.K., Batsford, 1960

LEARNING TO EMBROIDER
By Barbara Snook: U.K., Batsford, 1960; U.S.A., Hearthside Press,
1960

MACHINE EMBROIDERY
By Jennifer Gray: U.K., Batsford, 1963; U.S.A., Newman, 1963

100 EMBROIDERY STITCHES
Coats Sewing Group, 1962

Grateful thanks and acknowledgements are due to the following for their co-operation and help in the preparation of this
book: Coats Sewing Group; The Victoria and Albert Museum, London; The Metropolitan Museum of Art, New York;
The Humble Oil Refinery, Houston, Texas; Miss B. Sinclair Salmon and Miss L. DeDenne and The Embroiderers' Guild;
Jean Carter, Audrey Tucker and Members of the 1962 Group of the Embroiderers' Guild; Principal and students of
Whitelands College, Putney; Headmaster and pupils of Eliots Green Grammar School, Northolt, Middlesex; Headmaster
and pupils of Shepperton Green School, Shepperton, Middlesex; Mrs. D. Robinson; Gillian Hodgson; Marion D.
Hughes; Erian Short; Jean Baker; Pat Ross; Betty Fraser; Margaret Wiscombe. Dorothy, Steve and my parents.
Photography: D. A. E. Taylor, M.A., and Alan Wysman.

A

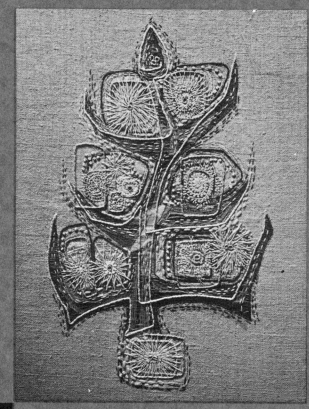

B

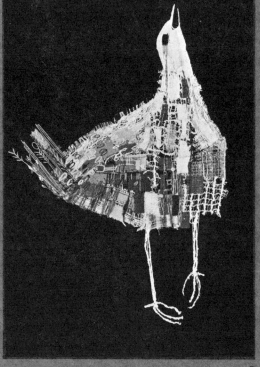

C

A. Animal—Chinese. (Embroiderers' Guild Collection).
B. Cross Section II. Linen, net and stitchery applied to hessian. (Jan Beaney).
C. Seagull. Applied nets and curtain fabrics. (Pat Ross).
D. Detail Syon Cope. English, late 13th century. Silk and silver-gilt threads. (Victoria and Albert Museum. Crown Copyright).
E. Detail from shawl — Indian. (Embroiderers' Guild Collection).
F. Woman's tunic. English, late 16th century. Some couched work. (Victoria and Albert Museum. Crown Copyright).

D

E

F